MY RECALLS

Milicent G. Tycko

authorHOUSE®

AuthorHouse™
1663 Liberty Drive
Bloomington, IN 47403
www.authorhouse.com
Phone: 1 (800) 839-8640

Published by AuthorHouse 10/10/2018

ISBN: 978-1-5462-6398-2 (sc)
ISBN: 978-1-5462-6397-5 (e)

Library of Congress Control Number: 2018912239

MY MAIN RECALL

MITZI WITH YOUNGER
BROTHER ARNOLD) I
LOVE HIM, SEE MY "BARET"
IN HAIR, I RECALL MY
SPECIAL YELLOW DRESS
WITH WHITE COLLAR. ARNOLD
IN IRONED (BY MOM) SHIRT

Chapter 1 MY REASONS

I WAS GOING TO CALL THIS BOOK: THIS IS ME OR WHO I AM. However, since I AM A 89 YEAROLD, EDUCATED LADY, I DECIDED IT WAS MORE APPROPRIATE TO CALL THIS BOOK: MY RECALLS

AS IS WELL KNOWN, OLDER PEOPLE SOMETIMES FORGET WHAT DAY IT WAS YESTERDAY, BUT DWELL ON OLD MEMORIES, OF CHILDHOOD, YOUNGSTERHOOD, AND NO EDITING IS INVOLVED, JUST A SPONTANEOUS HAPPENING. WHEN IT IS SAID "OLDER FOLKS", OVER 65 USUALLY MEANT, WELL, I AM MORE THAN "ELDERLY", I

AM ALMOST AT THE END,
A "SENIOR-SENIOR" AND SO
IT SEEMS APPROPRIATE TO
TITLE THIS BOOK "MY RECALLS".
THIS IS NOT INTENDED TO
GO DOWN IN A WILL TO
FAMILY YOUNGER GENERATIONS,
BUT IS ONLY A NATURAL
PLEASURE FOR ME NOW,
THE IMAGES, THOUGTS, PICTURE
IN MY MIND JUST FLOAT
ABOUT, NOT IN AN ORDERLY
FASHION, CORRECT OR NOT,
IT MATTERS NOT TO ME,
I AM ENJOYING THIS
INEVITABLE OCCURENCE,
MOSTLY IN EVENING,
SOMETIMES WAKES ME
IN MIDDLE OF THE NIGHT.

WHICH IS NOT TO SAY THAT I HAVE LOST SENSE OF REALITY. I AM WELL EDUCATED, A DOCTORAL IN CLINICAL PSYCHOLOGY, WORKED IN SCHOOLS AS ADMIRED CLINICAL SCHOOL PSYCHOLOGIST. I THINK MY UNDERSTANDINGS HELPED CHILDREN RELAX AND TALK TO ME. AS FOR REALITY, I AM MOTHER OF THREE GROWN ACCOMPLISHED SONS WHO VISIT US OFTEN. WHEN I SAY "US" I REFER TO MY 90 YEAR OLD INTELLIGENT HUSBAND — MARRIED TOGETHER 66 YEARS. HE IS RETIRED PHYSICS AND

COMPUTER PROFESSOR AT
STONY BROOK UNIVERSITY,
WHEN WE HAD OUR
HANDSOME AND BRILLIANT
THREE SONS, I WAS A
"STAY AT HOME" MOM.
I KNEW THEM AND HELPED
THEM GO THROUGH STAGES
OF THEIR LIFE, ALL EXCELLENT
STUDENTS AND PARTICIPATED
IN MUSIC PERFORMANCES
AT SCHOOL—THROUGH
HIGH SCHOOL, BECAME
SUCCESSFUL PROFESSIONALS
NICE WIVES AND FINALLY
I HAVE 6 GRANDCHILDREN
AND HAPPILY 4 ARE GIRLS.
MY HUSBAND AND ME LIVE

TOGETHER AND IT IS FUN AND HELPFUL THAT HE REMEMBERS A NAME, EVENT, THAT I FORGOT, AND VICE-VERSA. BEING DIFFERENT INTERESTS, PERSONALITIES, ALSO CREATES A HOME LIFE OF INTERESTS. HE DOES THE MATH, INCOME TAXES, ETC, AND I TALK TO OTHER PEOPLE WHO LOVE THIS, WHEN WE GO OUT TOGETHER, HE IS USUALLY MORE SILENT, UNLESS URGED TO CHAT, SO IT GOES. MANY OF OUR BELOVED FRIENDS AND FAMILY LONG PASSED AWAY. WE ARE LUCKY TO BE HERE STILL AT OUR AGES, AND REMEMBER THE DAYS GONE BY,

SO THIS EXPLAINS "MY RECALLS

CHAPTER 2
MY EARLY DAYS,
CHILDHOOD

THIS HAS BEEN FUN
TO "RECALL."

THE PHOTO OF ME WITH
MY YOUNGER BROTHER,
ARNOLD, WHO BECAME A
PROFESSIONAL TRUMPET
PLAYER, GROWN UP, PLAYED
IN CATSKILL HOTELS IN
SUMMER — BANDS WITH
OTHER MUSICIANS,
HE DIED AT AGE 76 YRS. I
MISS HIM SO MUCH NOW

GROWING UP AS A KID IN CITY
OF NEWARK WAS FUN, JUMP ROPE,
HOP SCOTCH WITH FRIENDS IN
NEIGHBORHOOD. RAN TO LOCAL
LIBRARIES TO BORROW MORE BOOKS,
ALWAYS HOME BY 5 O'CLOCK TO
BE WITH FAMILY REST OF DAY.

IN SCHOOL, TEACHERS RESPECTED
BY ALL PARENTS. WE HAD PENMAN-
SHIP DAILY, AND SPELLING TESTS EACH
WEEK, PUSH-PULLS AND OVALS
PRACTICED DAILY, TO IMPROVE
WRITING SKILLS. TEACHERS CHECKED
TO SEE IF OKAY. OTHERWISE WE
HAD TO REPEAT PAGE OF GOOD
PUSH-PULLS AND OVALS.

OF COURSE BY NOW, AN OLDER
89 YEAR OLD LADY, MY HAND-
WRITING HAS DETERIORATED.
SO "RECALLS" OF CHILDHOOD
PENMANSHIP AND SPELLING TESTS
ARE A DELIGHT FOR ME,

CHAPTER 3 - YOUNG ADULTHOOD

THOUGH BROUGHT UP BY MY MUSICAL CONCERT PIANIST MOTHER AND FATHER WHO WAS CANTOR IN NEWARK ORTHODOX SHUL — IT WAS THE ERA OF DEPRESSION AND THEY BOTH WORKED HARD FOR THE FAMILY.

NOBODY EXPECTED TO PUT THEIR KIDS THROUGH COLLEGE. BUT BEING BRIGHT, AND AMBITIOUS, I WORKED AT SUMMER JOBS TO MAKE AND SAVE MONEY. TOOK LYONS AVENUE BUS DOWNTOWN TO WORK AT KRESGE DEPARTMENT STORE. BUS COST ABOUT A NICKEL THEN.

I WAS ADMITTED TO THE LOCAL RUTGERS UNIVERSITY, AND MET THERE MANY OLDER MEN JUST RETURNED FROM THE WAR. THEY COULD DRIVE IN SECOND-HAND CARS AND OFTEN TOOK ME FOR A RIDE — IN RETURN FOR WHICH I CORRECTED THEIR PAPERS. I ENJOYED SINGING WITH MY GUITAR IN A CONTEST THERE

CHAPTER 3

I EXPECTED TO CONTINUE AT RUTGERS IN NEWARK, ALWAYS LIKED TO WRITE, BOOKS MY JOY, MY MOTHER WHO WAS BORN IN THIS COUNTRY, ALWAYS READ ME A STORY AT BEDTIME, MY FATHER WHO CAME HERE AS A CHILD, WITH MY "BUBBA" FROM UKRAINE, WITH 5 SIBLINGS, AND WAS A CANTOR IN SHUL IN NEARK, ALWAYS TOLD ME BEDTIME STORIES — SOMETIMES IN YIDDISH, OR HEBREW, OR HIS QUICKLY LEARNED ENGLISH, SO STORIES, WORDS, LANGUAGE, BOOKS WERE BIG PART OF MY GROWING UP. HOWEVER, WHEN A SOPHOMORE, MY PROFESSOR ADVISOR TOLD ME NOT TO MAJOR IN ENGLISH NEVER FIND A JOB, HE SAID, PICK ANOTHER EMPLOYABLE SUBJECT NOW. SO I DID, AND MAJORED IN PSYCHOLOGY, BIOLOGY. THIS CHOICE REMAINED AS I LATER WENT TO ANOTHER COLLEGE, UPSTATE, ANTHROPOLOGY, BIOLOGY, PSYCHOLOGY, ALL INTEREST-ING AND TOUGH COURSES, TAAUGHT BY EXPERT PROFESSORS, I PASSED COURSES — OF COURSE.

CHAPTER 4

Once upon a time I tried to write a rhyme   Each time I tried it was a bore   so I then

I started to snore   so....rhyme and time....and bore and snore

by M. Tycko

CHAPTER 4. YOUNG ADULTHOOD

I MET A YOUNG FRIEND, NOT A VET, WHO WAS SO SMART, WENT TO BRONX SCIENCE H.S. — SOON WILL GO UP TO COLLEGE AT CORNELL U., UPSTATE, HE TOOK ME AROUND PLACES IN NY — MY RUTGERS VETS DISAPPROVED — BUT INTERESTING ADVENTURE FOR ME. SAW THIRD AVE L — SEE PHOTO OF THIS OLD STRUCTURE ON NEXT PAGE, I DID, YES I DID GO UP TO CORNELL U. WITH HIM, MET NEW FRIENDS THERE — FROM SYRACUSE, ROCHESTER, TOOK MANY COURSES WITH FAMOUS PROFESSORS, IN PSYCOLOGY, ANTHROPOLOGY, BIOLOGY, A FEW FOR FUN, IN LITERATURE, HISTORY — MY WRITING LOVE, WITH YOUNG FRIEND WE HAD A WEEKLY RADIO FOR STUDENTS, SINGING AND PLAYING FOLK SONGS, THE LOCAL HOUSES WERE FOR STUDENTS, NO DORMS FOR US, LOVED THE SNOWY WINTERS, GREW UP IN NEWARK, MADE SNOWMEN

CHAPTER 5

OLDER NOW AND LOOKING BACK — AS "ELDERLY" TEND TO DO. I "RECALL" MY YOUNG GRANDCHILDREN YEARS AGO — SONIA AND JOSHUA. AT NIGHT I OFTEN "RECALL" WHEN THEY WERE YOUNG. I "RECALL" OFTEN TAKING CARE, HAPPILY, OF THESE KIDS.

SEE EARLY PHOTO NEXT PAGE. THEN SEE THEM ON RECENT VISIT TO US THIS WEEK. THEY INSISTED ON "GROWING UP". I INSISTED ON BECOMING THEIR MUCH LOVED "ELDERLY" GRANDMA.

→

CHAPTER 5:
"RECALL" GRANDKIDS WHEN YOUNGSTERS

HOWEVER LOVE THEM ALWAYS NOW WHEN THEY ARE BRIGHT AND GROWN TO BE ACCOMPLISHED ADULTS, JOSHUA A GENETICIST. TRAVELS ALL AROUND

WORLD. HERE AS I LIKE TO "RECALL", IS JOSUA IN RED JUMPER. OLDER SISTER SONIA WORKS FOR DOCTORAL DEGREE NOW AT HARVARD U. THEIR MOM, CAROL TYCKO, VISITED US RECENTLY. MITZI—WELL HAIR NOW GREY

CHAPTER 5:

MOTHER CAROL WITH JOSHUA NOW,
GREW UP BRIGHT, HANDSOME, TALL
AND CONSIDERATE. HE HELPS ME
NOW, HIS "ELDEALY" GREY HAIRED
GRANDMA GET IN AND OUT OF THE
CAR, OPENS DOOR FOR ME. P.S.
ALSO HELPS MY HUSBAND DAN,
AGE 90 YRS., GET OUT OF CAR, ETCETERA.
CAROL AND JOSHUA NOW SIT IN OUR
DEN, AND SMILE TO BE VISITING US.
CAROL NOW WEARS EYE-GLASSES
M. Jycko

JOSHUA LIVES FAR FROM NJ,
IN HIS CALIFORNIA APARTMENT,
AND DOES NOTABLE RESEARCH IN
GENETICS.

CHAPTER 6   FAMILY AND FRIENDS

AS IN THE PREFACE, I MOST "RECALL" WHEN MY BROTHER ARNOLD AND I WERE YOUNG CHILDREN OUR MOTHER, A CONCERT PIANIST, BORN IN USA, AND MY FATHER, AN ORTHODOX KANTOR BROUGHT THROUGH ELLIS ISLAND BY MY "BUBBA" WITH 6 SURVIVING CHILDREN, FROM SHTETL IN UKRAINE, MY GRANDFATHER, A FURRIER, DID NOT SURVIVE PNEUMONIA AND NEVER CAME HERE, "BUBBA" HAD 12 CHILDREN, ONLY 6 SURVIVED, NO TREATMENTS IN UKRAINE BACK THERE, THEY LIVED NEAR THE SEA THERE, AND MY FATHER AS A CHILD WAS GOOD SINGER AND WENT WITH A SINGING GROUP AROUND UKRAINE, HE WAS ALWAYS MUSICAL — LATER IN HIS LIFE HE ALWAYS MISSES HIS FATHER, SOME PHOTOS OF SHUL AND

CHAPTER 6 FAMILY AND FRIENDS

IN NEWARK, MANY JEWISH EMIGRANTS CAME, ARE FOLLOWING. LATER ON NEWARK CHANGED — MANY MOVED TO MAPLEWOOD, DOWN TO LAKEWOOD. PHOTOS FOLLOW OF "SHUL" BEFORE IT LATER BECAME A BAPTIST CHURCH.

MY FAMILY IN LAKEWOOD, MY FATHER OFTEN MET OTHERS THERE AND COULD SPEAK TO THEM IN YIDDISH, HEBREW, RUSSIAN, ENGLISH HE WAS ALWAYS FRIENDLY, HAD PHRASES I "RECALL". HE DID NOT LIKE THOSE WHO "KVETCHED", COMPLAINED, ABOUT EVERY MINOR ACHE AND PAIN AND PROBLEM. "YUSL", MY FATHER JOSEPH GERMANSKY SAID "ONLY ONE THING INEVITABLE" THAT IS DEATH. I MISS HIM SO MUCH AND OFTEN "RECALL" HIM.

CHAPTER 6   FAMILY AND FRIENDS

THIS MY OLDEST GRANDDAUGHTER

SONIA TYCKO

REMEMBER WHEN A CHILD READING
A BOOK, NEXT TO BROTHER JOSHUA IN
FORMER CHAPTER. SONIA ALWAYS
ARTISTIC—MANY OF HER DRAWINGS
AND PAINTINGS LINE OUR ENTRANCE
HALL—FROM WHEN SHE WAS YOUNGER.
HERE I HAPPILY "RECALL" GIVING TO
HER THIS ANTIQUE RUSSIAN DOLL FROM
OUR HIGH BOOK-CASE SHELF. SHE
ADMIRED THE BEAUTY, AND WITHIN ARE
SMALLER AND SMALLER LITTLE DOLLS. SO
I GAVE THIS TO SONIA, KNOWING SHE
WOULD ALWAYS TAKE CARE OF IT. I
"RECALL" THIS PHOTO FROM SEVERAL YEARS
AGO—I AM GREY-HAIRED ELDERLY—OUTSIDE
ON OUR DECK. SONIA STUDIES EARLY AMERICAN
HISTORY, FOR DOCTORAL AT HARVARD U. GOES
TO UK TO USE MANY ARCHIVES. NOW FINISHING
WRITING THESIS—WITH FRIEND JOE, IN PHILLY.

JOE STUDIES EARLY FRENCH HISTORY.

IN LAKEWOOD AFTER
LEAVING NEWARK

CHAPTER 6 FAMILY AND FRIENDS

"RECALL" FATHER CANTOR IN
ORTHODOX NEWARK "SHUL"

NOW WE VISIT KOSHE ZAMS
FOR MEAL WITH CAROL AND JOSHUA
FATHER GONE - BUT REMEMBERED. HE
WOULD LIKE TO BE WITH US.

CHAPTER 6   FAMILY AND FRIENDS

PAINTING BY MY
MOTHER — LONG PASSED AWAY — KEEP
ON ENTRANCE HALL WALL

CHAPTER 6   FAMILY AND FRIENDS

PASSED AWAY—MY DEAR
FRIEND SHIRLEY LEVY—MISS HER.

BURIAL OF MY BELOVED PET,BORDER
COLLIE "PRINCESS"— HAD HER UNDERSTANDING
FRIENDSHIP FOR 11 YEARS—MISS HER A LOT,

CHAPTER 6 FAMILY AND FRIENDS

THE LEICHTLING SIDE (MY MOTHER DAISY LEICHTLING GERMANSKY) IS IMPORTANT.

OLDER COUSINS, ALICE MORLEY, TOM PALEY, AND I ALWAYS WENT UP TO KERHONKSON IN SUMMERS, TO BE WITH GRANDMA MINNIE AND GRANDPA ADOLF LEICHTLING. SO MANY HAPPY MEMORIES. OUR UNCLE MAX STILL THERE AND TOOK US FOR RIDES IN THE 'RUMBLE SEAT' OF HIS CAR. THEN HE WAS DRAFTED, WW2, INTO NAVY. GRANDMA MINNIE DIED, FEW YEARS LATER GRANDPA ADOLF DIED. TOM PALEY, FAMOUS FOLKSINGER DIED. ALICE MORLEY'S OLDER BROTHER RICHARD SHOT DOWN IN WAR - AIR CRAFT. LATER HOME HE LIKED TO READ BOOKS BUT GOT LOST WALKING AROUND NEIGHBORHOOD.

UNCLE MAX MARRIED ANN AND THEY HAD A STORE IN LOWER MANHATTAN. THEIR SON, ALAN VERY MUSICAL, WENT TO JULLIARD, THEN COMPOSED SONATAS, CONDUCTED ORCHESTRAS. HE BECAME ORTHODOX, SENT HIS GIRLS TO HEBREW SCHOOL, AVROHOM LIVES WITH OTHER ORTHODOX JEWS AND ALSO GOES TO LAKEWOOD TO SET UP SCHOOLS FOR ORTHODOX STUDENTS. COUSIN MAGGIE PALEY TOM'S YOUNGER SISTER LIVES IN NY, EDITS BOOKS, A JOURNALIST, WROTE A GOOD BOOK WHICH I READ.

SO, I "RECALL" OLDER DAYS UP IN KER HONKSON, OFTEN TALK ABOUT TO COUSIN ALICE MORLEY.
MAGGIE AND AVRO HOM TOO YOUNG, NOT THERE

CHAPTER 7   MY WRITINGS

Upon Hearing Mozart's Divertimento for Violin, Viola and Cello

Trio

Viola

It is bleak in the forest that I go through. The trees appear
to be hung like black cardboard lanterns in oily and licorice
profusion. There is no acquittal from this somber, cavernous
woods. Brambled pathways wind about the trees as rasping viola
phrases straining to sing in shadowy, muted, and nightmare-blunted
cries. It is forever pre-dawn. The forest scurryings have
lost their urgent edge and rustle, blunted now into a hushed
and mournful wait. Darkness is prolonged, the prose of nature halted.

Cello

Mabel Salmon in her mercerized cotton plaid exploded brightly in
the streets, never being sad. She had a good time night and a
razzle flashing grin, and it was welcome, welcome, welcome halle-
lujah world. Like a shiny glowing cello with its curves intact,
she opened up a furrow through the turbid air. Oval and glorious,
supple and sane, her sonorous way was knuckled along in grace.

Violin

A consumer par excellence, briefcase in hand, wended his way
at noon over regular slates that glistened like wind-washed,
watery stones. Regularized, geometrized and paced accordingly,
he let himself reflect the building grids of windows and walls,
as an inverse waffle. His right-angled way into restaurant and
shops was eased by doormen near doorsteps. Glancing on displays ,
as a violin in clarity, his walk flowed on. It figured promi-
nently in no headlines, yet in innocence and speed, it sang
out surely and was comfortable, confined in range. Glissando round
a corner, embraced by outside chaos, the line of march was
stranger to all doubt. Sidewalks paced in intervals for hard-
cash purchase purposes, formed taut-stringed streets to play
upon; his violin city.

And so the trio ended, we applauded, and we left.

1977

Summer Wanderings

A cow is lazy and incumbent
not insolvent though
because of its milk assets

but incumbent as it
stands upon its grassy slope
displaying mass in white and black
solidified in trance

incumbent as it sits in shade
confusing with its white and black
the gleam and gloom of shadows

all toward regally possessing space in shape of cow
unseatable and stolid now.

a furzed farm under
rainbow glass
        water drop
enlarging wheat
enlarging grains
enlarging crawling
buzzing bugs
enlarging spiked leaves
enlarging sticky stalks
        clear beauty under
rainbow glass
        softly rippling
velvet growth of pulsing farm

cornea captured
sweetened by bees
colored by birds
made gaudy by
eggplants and berries
        and grapes
seen large under glass

as the blood in the
seed of pomegranate fruit
is shielded and sought
through translucent hard walls.

February Self

Sometimes I float obliquely through the fog
But otherwise
I try for logarithmic sails
Above the snow-patched fields
And other farm-like
Attributes of earth
Mainly to avail myself
Of sadness in its liquid state.

Then within
There lies a sodden doom
A mood of undislodgeable and moor-like mass

The lost   the unforgiven

Small raindrops tinkling on the glass of my soul
Provide a melody of counteracting song
In which I seek delight and find
Liquid lyrics which succeed in
Separating me from self.

A semi-detached mind gazes on curtains blown
Merely gauze billowing between earth and self
As bandages laid
Caressingly on wounds.

It is said:
Send no message
Send no note.

A song exists sailed fleetingly by hands
As paper folded formed in youth
Though dampened now by fog
Or is it tears?

It can be said:
Not a message but a poem obliquely floats
Crying out in noteless voice
Obedient yet sung.

A semi-detached mind gazes on curtains lilting
Merely gauze billowing between earth and self
As bandages laid
Caressingly on sounds
Caressingly on wounds
Assuaging fitful pain as parts approach.

Obedient and melancholy all the earth lies fitfully
Beneath the snow
And tries to sing itself to sleep
Without a message or a note.

Infrequently yet blessedly
The slanted rain draws sadness out
Enabling mood to crystallize upon each drop
Alleviating gloom.

Cut not:
Wrong not:
Hurt not:
Lose not:
Cry not:
Wail not:
Weep not:
Be not:
Write not:
Sing not:
Send not:

So states the rain   so states the snow   so states the fog
So states the wound   so states the sound   so states the word

Released in song the noteless voice permits itself
Yet cannot.

Obedient and melancholy all the earth lies fitfully
Beneath the snow
And tries to sing itself to sleep
Without a message or a note.

1983

Milicent Tycko

February Elegy

For this very February bemoaned and
Restless in leafy edged sadness
For the decade of pond wooded snows
Window gazed in thought

For this very February as summer and
Always continuing wintry spring
Out of season now
Belated and curiously present with
Aged grasshoppers stretched in
Useless strivings upon
Long lying brown and wet logs long lain in fixed
Patterns caught in leafy snow and etching light

A steadiness does prevail though leaf
Quivering restless and too sad
For words for
Grasshoppers feeble yet
Assigned to work
They cannot do.

Desolate logs long lain in silent woods
During February summers and summer itself
As drawn in chalky waves of grey.

The woods remain therefore cross-hatched in trees
Yes though the breath of little ones no longer
Adds to mist of pond and leaf decay
The pattern lives.

It seems the trees are ultimate groom and ultimate bride

Through whose fingers ran the breath of child and sigh of age
Through whose long and lying logs and sad crisp leaves
The lichened tears of fungal white lie shed and ghastly still .

                                          1983
                                    Milicent Tycko

Wandering in Books

Milicent Tycko

    A dusty bookcase beckoned a broom, so one
dark wintry day I determined to delve into the
heretofore undisturbed array of books jamming
my shelves for many years. Quite a few were still in
orderly alignment, straight up with their jackets displayed
regularly and in roughly size place. These were probably the
ones which had been found least interesting and were
silently retaining their place, as dinosaurs permanently
arranged, by compulsive curators, in glass cases.
Then there popped into view the extra tall books
which could never stand up straight and preferred to lie
langorously on top of the unread orderly straight up books.

    Not so simple for the overabundance of interesting
books acquired from month to month or year to
year in spite of resolutions not to impact limited
space. Irresistible and each one at least temporarily
outstanding, this motley conglomeration piled itself
high in stacks atop the bookcase, and admittedly also
in stacks atop other furniture…dressers, desks, tables
and chairs, but never on floors.
    The consummate challenge was to keep one's brain
functioning as a card catalog which could easily locate a
book or prevent the same one from being purchased anew.
    This plethora of books became a cozy cradle
surrounding my space and was easily imagined to
be a colorful abstract painting. The authors cried out
sometimes at night and competed loquaciously for
attention and, truth be known, their styles and subjects
seemed to be affected by outside events which shifted
and sieved their inherent interest.
    Aside from obvious outside events in history which
changed their interest for me, admittedly there were
gradually changing internal conditions which affected their use.
As arthritis set in, somehow the heavier and taller books became
neglected in favor of smaller almost booklet sized tomes.
The formerly fascinating 734 page book became very
tedious and verbose. Sight itself became a greater issue
and dim lighted days versus modulated sunny days seemed
to influence literary judgment unduly. Memory discrepancies
became a two edged sword, because one could re-read
text with a feeling of fresh discovery. It certainly

Now I can dwell upon the meaning of it all.

Perimeters

A perimeter exists along the parrot's wing
Up around the part that does attempt to sing
The throat that gabbles crumbs to caw
A sound remote, no matter for I saw
The line continue round the feathered form
Encasing all its puffy green and bright
Markings cleanly right before my sight

Exactly, and I felt perimeters proclaim
To be available upon the edge of all the sea
But breathless lines could not regain
Stability, the foam at beach's shore
Though light and bubbly where it crept
Destroyed with ease and to the core
My concept
Of perimeters, it flowed in daring
Dashes toward the beach, the sea
So ruminating ceaselessly from deep
And tireless moans
With waves capped moonlit each.

Seeking once again to draw perimeters
My eyes alight on pebbles moist
Trod upon by sea-wrens, gulls and mussel-heaps
All choked by weeds from sea and kelp
There stay the smoothened rocks
Certainly a line defines each stone
For one appears a tan and white elongate egg
Seen in border circumspect
Apart and hard, as you and I
Forget the sea, its surging and
Its openness.

Waves flow
As separate stones lie on sand
In cool radiance almost
Cold
Their skins glow
From salt spray
Cast upon them.

We took a break
In Greenport in the little store
Along the harbor side
There was a large straw basket
Filled with puffin toys of fake fur
Black and white with thickened beaks
Set upon the floor

Then we two stepped out
Escaping soap and candle smells
Into the real sea-cleared air
Where a seagull stood upon
The planks of wood there
Its grey and stiffened wings
Hardly ruffled in the spray

It hurt my eyes to my surprise

The sea
The bird unheard
The sea
Is roaring loudly
Why?
Its salty fingers permeate already
Bird
Why drown it out?

(Continues later)

Disjointed visions as I tried
To demarcate in innocence
The meanings of perimeters
All along the salt drenched shore

Contrasting with those puffin toys
Within that tiny store for naught
My mind saw ships of boys afloat
Towards battles grim on foreign soil
Rushing ceaselessly to join
In gunny turmoil
While the planks of wood
And broken glass were swiftly sent
Along the frothy edge of ocean's pulse.

Overhead the seagull flies
And cries out clear
Its vessels vials
Of sea spray too
As are the calling ospreys'

Demarcated now in gloom
Persistent as the pulse of waves
The concept of perimeters
Reaches far and deeper still

Lying moist on foreign strands
As pebbles black and white
The boys are lying silently
Sublime
Defined at last
Perimeters

Linen Fragments

More intricate my love I cannot be
Embroidering my wishes on a sorrow tree
Of time spent otherwise in empty ways
Sewn images in floss old memories in haze
Preserved as linen fragments in Egyptian tombs
Locked past touch in glass museum wombs

Were my thoughts to be spoken with hesitant breath
Their layered pattern would soon dissolve in death
The loosening of their threads would rasp along the hall
Where cool museum cases float in still sonic pall
More intricate my suffering more silent too
It cannot be while played upon by words from you.

1986 Millicent Tycko

The Octopus in October

In October an Octopus deftly
Sidled along the
Silky bottom of the large
And sumptuous sea

Forlorn as only he could
Sense the emptiness of the
Sea filled with glowing forms
Of fish and weed yet
Powerless in spite of
Its immensity

To bring its Octopi
The brilliant colors violet
And red and vivid yellow on
Gauguin painted leaves
Those colors dazzling in a
Shameless way the ones who
Emigrated to museums recently
From the sea
So being declared an animal
Of wit and thoughtful mind
In October an Octopus despairingly
Felt like crying for its kind
Doomed to living in dark sea-caves
Though artistically inclined

The Fish in the Dish

A fish in scaley armor
Lay gasping on the plate
It wriggled and fluttered its gills
As it muttered "I think I prefer to not wait"
"better not to wait"

Our Love is a Planet

Our love is a planet
Which leads us in
Calculated arcs
Near starry sequels as all the
Heavens surrounding whirl

Long ago a whisper of love
Established the core of heat
No matter what layers
Of crystallized ice do
Intervene often
In shells of time

The spin was determined
And veers not awry
Forever returning and
Circling anew
In love's parabolic design

1986 Milicent Tycko

Frog Poem

The little frog pulsing and moist
It looked at me as I held it in my palm
Then leapt away, I loved it so.

Later I held a pink carnellian frog
Carved glossy and cold upon my palm
It sat in weighty silence, I admired it so.

Since our breath-ringed love
Must fade awash in tears someday
I write this poem
To freeze our moments still, I wish it so.

                                    1986
                              Milicent Tycko

Moth Poem

Exist I brown in abstract gloom
A moth wing dusty and detached
Adheres to my shoe
And I lift it lightly
If only to
Examine striations
Of archaeological
Tan admixtured with
Bands of brown.

1986
Milicent Tycko

Shore Willow

Who knows what life is all about
The much-sketched owl sits plumply on
His roughened bough affirming with alacrity
His wonder and bewilderment

In stasis and benumbed
The space abounds with busy flocks
Of birds who whirl about in puzzlement
Flashing as they dart the
Yellow-bright of underwing
Or in a duller raiment singing wondrous songs

Or thin blue-bodied dragon-flies
Weaving in their flight a knotted path
Of shadow blue
In amongst the lilac leaves so smooth
And placid green that hang in simple shapes
Underneath the waving willow stems
That we two lie beneath in order
That we may pretend to be alone in
Canopied protection as we take delight
In dancing movements of the pale green leaves
Which shield us as a coverlet so
We may lie upon this grass together
And forever in a timeless Breughel scene

All geese flow together in their radiance
Of pattern as if seeking anonymity
And gaining it by fleeing cold together
In eternal noisy travels
Skyfuls of geese, as we
Are puzzled too by furious forces
Ignorant of how to flee
For love does bind us in our
Twoness underneath the willow house
And all we ever need or wanted there
Ends in our embrace.

1986 Milicent Tycko

Distances

I see before me reaching out a great and open plain
With no disdain to mar its velvet honeyed cover offering
Lark ways undisturbed by sphynxes only wheat
As sand unending beckons birds and unheard gusts of air
For wideness does prevail beyond the chant of wings whirred there

Vast quiet follows pulsing (pulling) of the sea
Wet wind often slashes salt in glistening threnody.

                                        1987   Milicent Tycko

CHAPTER 7 MY WRITINGS

NOT ONLY POEMS, STORIES.
WHEN I LOOK UP NOW AT
CLOUDS, I SEE FORMS, LIKE
DOGS, LAKES, SNAKES, CONTINENTS.
AS DO OTHERS PROBABLY.

BUT THEN I "RECALL" MANY
DECADES AGO, WHEN I WROTE
MY DOCTORAL THESIS ON RORSHACK
RESPONES, IN GRADUATE SCHOOL. I
"RECALL" MY HELPFUL PROFESSOR,
OTHER GRADUATE STUDENTS, SOME
AS FRIEND GLORIA FRANKLIN, WHO SINCE
PASSED AWAY.

MY THESIS ON RORSHACK RESPONSES
WAS PUBLISHED, CAN READ, BY
MILICENT G. TYCKO.

OR JUST HAVE FUN LOOKING
FOR DOGGIES UP IN THE CLOUDS.

Our Love is a Planet

Our love is a planet
Which leads us in
Calculated arcs
Near starry sequels as all the
Heavens surrounding whirl

Long ago a whisper of love
Established the core of heat
No matter what layers
Of crystallized ice do
Intervene often
In shells of time

The spin was determined
And veers not awry
Forever returning and
Circling anew
In love's parabolic design

1986 Milicent Tycko

Perceptual and Motor Skills, 1959, 9, 167-180. © Southern Universities Press 1959

RORSCHACH RESPONSES AT FOUR EXPOSURE LEVELS[1]

MILICENT TYCKO

Irvington-on-Hudson, New York

The purpose of the present study was to further clarify the role of stimulus exposure time as a variable which affects responses to projective material. Presentation of the standard Rorschach cards over a series of exposure times, ranging from .03 sec. to unlimited exposure, constituted a systematically controlled range of perceptual conditions with stimuli known to have rich and useful personality correlates. In an earlier tachistoscopic study Stein (1949) demonstrated different patterns of response as a function of exposure time of Rorschach cards; however, the small sample used (17 *Ss* who responded under ascending exposure order) limited the generality of his results, and no evaluation of perceptual modes, independent of the experimental conditions, was reported. Stein's study explored the clinical usefulness of a tachistoscopic Rorschach technique by applying it to the analysis of several individual cases. A later study by Stein and Meer (1954) pointed to the usefulness of the tachistoscopic Rorschach technique in discriminating between *Ss* of high and low creative ability.

In the view of this author, the experimental design used in the present study invites consideration of what perceptual processes may accompany the physically manipulated conditions of minimal and sustained exposure of the stimulus. When an external stimulus is exposed very briefly, the opportunity for the perceiver to base his reactions on an interaction with the stimulus is relatively limited, and he is thereby forced to rely largely upon subjective factors and his immediate, brief perception of the stimulus. Some of the contributing factors which the perceiver may bring to the experimental situation are those of cognitive structure, personality structure, motivational states, and past learning. As exposure time of the external stimulus is increased, more time is available during which interaction between perceiver and stimulus can occur. As there is increased opportunity to investigate the stimulus at slower tachistoscopic speeds, more information can be obtained from the stimulus, and there is more time for corrections in perception. While the experimental situation thus varies systematically in the opportunity for interaction, it does nor of course follow that all *Ss* will respond equally to the increased possibilities for interaction with the stimulus at longer exposure times. The present article will be limited to a report and discussion of the more formal aspects of Ror-

[1] This article is based upon a doctoral dissertation submitted in partial fulfillment of the requirements for the degree of Doctor of Philosophy in the School of Education of New York University, 1956. The author is indebted to Professor John J. Sullivan for his direction of the research. An abridged account of the study was presented at the Sixty-Sixth Annual Convention of the American Psychological Association, 1958.

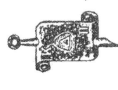

(CHAPTER 8   MY TRAVELS (PREFACE)
          (WRITTEN 9/10/2018)
  I "RECALL" WAY BACK THAT MY FATHER
DROVE US THROUGH THE HOLLAND TUNNEL
TO GET TO VISIT OUR RELATIVES IN
BROOKLYN. BUT MUCH LATER, I "RECALL"
THE BUILDING OF LINCOLN TUNNEL AND
THEN THE HIGH UP WITH GORGEOUS VIEWS,
THE GEORGE WASHINTON BRIDGE. MY
FATHER, WHO CAME TO USA FROM UKRAINE HAD TO LEARN
WHO GEORGE WASHINTON WAS. BUT—AN
EXPANSIVE, AND EXPENSIVE TO BUILD,
GEORGE WASHINGTON BRIDGE? HE
DROVE US ACROSS AND A THRILL FOR
ALL OF US. WE KNEW OUR FATHER,
JOSEPH GERMANSKY, WAS A GOOD EXPERIENCED
DRIVER. NOW I "RECALL" THAT SOMETIMES
ONLY ONE LANE WAS OPEN — CONSTRUCTION,
REPAIRS, EVENTUALLY THEREFORE A NEW
BRIDGE ACROSS HUDSON RIVER, WAS BUILT,
TAPPAN ZEE (SP.?) AND FURTHER NORTH,
EASY TO REACH FROM WESTCHESTER, NY,
AND GOING BACK SOUTH TO NEWARK,
WHERE MOST OF FAMILY STILL LIVED, COULD
EVEN DRIVE A FEW MORE MILES TO ELIZABETH NJ,
WHERE MY MOTHER DAISY LEICHTLING WAS
BORN — IN USA. BUT TODAY THE RADIO SAYS
THAT TAPPAN ZEE IS BEING DEMOLISHED.
INSTEAD TAKE NEW MODERN MARIO COMO
BRIDGE, NAMED BY HIS SON ANDREW COMO IN
TRIBUTE TO HIS LONG-TIME EXCELLENT
GOVERNOR OF NY STATE, HIS FATHER,
BUT—PRESENT GOVERNOR, ANDREW COMO IS
NOT MARRIED. HAPPY ROSHASHONAH, M. TYCKO

CHAPTER 8
MY TRAVELS

THEN, WAY BACK THEN, NOW

Milicent Tycko, July 2008

THEN, WAY BACK THEN, NOW

THEN would be a way of ordering a lot of written notes, diaries,
mementos that took up space in a desk drawer which started to reek of
non-wondrous aromas, like moldy spider legs and moist-blotched differentially
decaying papers, cardboards and plastic covers. THEN, might, once investigated,
comprise years from around 1985 to early 2000s.

WAY BACK THEN, would be a way of roughly distancing generations, as in a
genealogical survey. This might comprise papers only slightly becoming beige,
not actually turning yellow, and also recordings on floppy discs and CDs.

NOW, would be a semantic guise to indicate current events and thoughts,
but would of course have to include all of THEN and WAY BACK THEN which enter
into the underlying selective perception of what is NOW., different NOWS for
different days, hours, moods, thoughts ,interpersonal relations..

The above orderly sounding introduction is, by confession, only a fumbling
attempt to stall the project. In honesty, the feeble motivation for trying to
look upon the task as a literary assignment, is a cover up for a simple house-
keeping unpleasant task. Namely to sort through loads of saved words so that
they can be tossed out and make room in the desk drawers, the shelf surfaces, the
notebook covers, the computer hard drives, the rooms, the house, the yard and
garden and all else so that it would seem that a united clean sweep was a mystery as
to what had constituted all the dentritus heretofore. The title of this could have been
just the word ME, but there already is this book, or maybe VACUUM CLEANER
BAG or maybe TIME to get the house ready to sell to buyers who want to impose
their own imagination on the space and layout of the rooms. We are told, and
this sentence belongs to the NOW part, that curb appeal is important when there is a
surfeit of homes for sale.

Picked up a Museum of Modern Art Calendar 1985 booklet which I bought
back THEN.. My favorite, from when MOMA was an old building connected by
a threshold to the old Whitney museum, is the Henri Rousseau painting called\
Sleeping Gypsy, an oil from 1897. So, right away, I see that the THEN category
really encompasses the WAY BACK THEN category, which will probably keep
adding depth and interest to everything. A pretty cool gimic, as my NOW grandson
would say.. A Calder work called Morning Star, 1943, a scene with Mae Clarke and
James Cagney in Public Enemy, Warner Bros., 1931, an etching by Edvard Munch
The Morning After, 1895, and on the page for September, the inevitable Vincent van
Gogh The Starry Night, 1889, across from the blank diary page for September 9, 10,
11, 12…and further, all of which were left blank by me, only in large script saying
Trip on Canadian National Railroad This was the trip Dan, Jonathan and I took
through Canadian scenery to Vancouver, where we met Robert, toured and then
went to San Francisco, when he was at Berkeley.. (A later Amtrak tour. .. referred to our
trip across country by train, to Chicago,
St. Louis, New Mexico, Los Angeles, and finally San Francisco. We took this
trip to visit our oldest son Benjamin and wife Carol. He went there to do medicall

residency work at Stanford U). If this brief mention of the 1985 booklet would end here, enough memories would be included. However, unfortunately I had already removed many of the earlier diary pages from the booklet, the ones with my handwriting filling up many of the dates in many other months, so the THEN has to become more personalized. Remember that after skimming through these, the beige to yellow pages will actually go to the garbage collection, making much more space in the empty drawer.

Since these pages were not kept in calendar order, the contents will also be a rough semblance of that year, and could be called a SKIMMED PASTICHE. Our youngest son Jonathan was about 17 years and some of his high school days and ensuing early college days are there, and his older brother Robert, in college and beyond, was frequently visiting with us. In fact, I wrote on the 16th, "..spoke to Robert who told me he was invited to the prestigious Gordon conference in June, as an expert on NMR."And the next day, the 17th I wrote,"Snow day. 5 inches of lovely white and

Jonathan and I had a quiet day at home. He shoveled the driveway for me. Dan came home safely in late afternoon. Cooped up in house." on the 18th,"Today very cold again. Went to do shopping for store of food before next storm. Jonathan came home and he was happy to have been given the part of Reverand Hale in 'The Crucible'" The 19th…."snow type day at home on 16th "Enjoyed meeting Robert in city and we all went to Alice Tully Hall for a harpsichord concert. The 17th,"Nice quiet day at home. Made huge turkey dinner " The 31st," Robert came to visit for a couple of days Jonathan has relaxing week off from school. 'like one long sigh' he says contentedly. He is writing a play. Robert met Jean in NYC to see Noel Coward play…Ben staying to work in Palo Alto..took walk at beach….had lovely family New Years Day and then drove into NYC in heavy fog to take Rob to Penn Sta. Dan and I walked on Fifth Ave, buildings were gauzy and ethereal in mist, very warm, amiable crowd, ate in Wolffs and drove home silencing woods with ermine wraps on evergreens, (wow)…Came home where Jonathan finishing his play called 'Fade to Dark.''.
On 8,9,10,11,12," We did some business in Hempstead then took walk at beach where Very wild wind whipped. Had nice day with Jonathan home for warming beef stew, then off to his Wind Ensemble. Tomorrow Dan goes for 3 days to Technicon and I clean house. Very cold out, the rhododendron leaves are as tightly closed as cigars. Had home day, did many chores. Jonathan had relaxing afternoon and we got to talk in evening. He is very verbal and sophisticated and introspective and complex by now. Freezing out. Will have lunch out if car starts. Right side still hurts below rib area. Must check it out soon…Mary Leakey's autobiography finished.
On 14th,"Will go swimming. Yesterday's walks helped us both a lot. While aching, am glad…" 15th,"had horrible time on Montauk trip. A lot of silence and stupidity from Dan. He drove out of way so were in car for about 5 hrs. Had 20 minute swim…then overate at home due to misery about my life. ..waste 33 years on an idiot…"(NOW please note that the number has become 57 years, so some good stuff must have overall compensated…I guess).
21st,"Freezing out, howling wind. Jack Frost worked on windows last night. At least

Jonathan has a day home from school to sleep late. He painted his room yesterday, which is nice" 28th,"Sent a plant to Daisy and Joe for their 57th anniversary. They called to say they loved it. Both quite alert and well" 31st," Snowflakes again. Past days
uneventful. Jon home late from his Crucible rehearsals. Gave him permission for ski trip to Bellayre Feb. 9 with school. Where's my Dan?"

Feb. 6," Snow day, no school. Awoke to very thickly covered landscape. "7th,"Ballet evening...wonderful day. Dan and I walked through many areas of NYC, from Lincoln Ctr, down 9th Ave...across 34th and almost all back, to see the lovely Leibesleider Walzer again of City Ballet. Delightful day for us." 8th," Windy and cold. Prepared for Jonathan's ski trip to Bellayre. He leaves 4:30 am tomorrow with his high school bus. Hope the wind doesn't blow him down. Nervous but glad for him. Bought makings of his birthday cake." 9th,"Dan and I up at 3 am to take Jon in dark and cold to the high school
to meet the ski trip bus. Very freezing windy day. Were we glad to get him home by 9:30 pm...safe and sound...and he loved the skiing." 10"Slept late then had a good walk at beach. Dan, I and Jonathan had lovely birthday party with champagne, linguini and home made chocolate cake for Jonathan. It was pleasant for all. He likes his presents." 11th,"Wonderful milder day today. I walk the village streets, crying inside, as I think of all the phases of Jonathan's life here...so long ago..I wheeled his stroller to the salty seaside..he has been a dear...seems yester now he is 17 yrs old. Glad we are here to see him as a wonderful young man.,.smart, sensitive, talented and warm. Hopefully Dan and I will see him launched in his life's work 4 or 5 years from now..whatever that may be. He is a versatile person" 15th,"Dan hurt his head. Nine stitches at Mather. Really bad day, frightening for me. That's only part of it." 16th,"Robert visited for lovely weekend at home. Healing get together." 17th," Went to beach, all of us. Nice dinner at home. Nice visit with Rob. Had phone call from Ben also".

March 7th,"Wonderful performance by Jonathan...very strong voice, lots of subtle modulation" 9th,"Played to packed houses Fri. and Sat. (Crucible WMHS) He is glad its over, was a grueling play to do" 25th,"Ben bought condo in Palo Alto. Hope he loves it. Good to hear him happy." 26th"Sad to hear Iz Elster (LA) passed away."
16th,"We called Ben and asked him to arrange his May trip to give us the week-end when we are free. He can't come to Jon's graduation in June...blue about this. What's a family anyhow? Dan very annoyed also. Will try to forget it all."

April 18th,"Trip to Ithaca. Jon drove some. enjoyed re-visiting Cornell campus while Jon went to admissions open houses. " 19th,"Misty rain in Ithaca, saw gorges, museum, Dan saw Ken King, ate in Statler, had pleasant trip, enjoyed the ornithology area...Jon finds it not exactly for him I think."
22nd,"Plesant visit to Baltimore, Cross Keys Inn, well impressed by faculty, goals, of Johns Hopkins U. 25th,"Jonathan decided to accept admissions to Hopkins in Baltimore staring Sept. 85. Good luck my dear sweet child. Hope to be at your B.A. graduation in May 89   (We were there when he graduated, and also when he gothis law degree later at Columbia Law School...so life went ahead) . May 11th," Met Ben and Carol in city at Harley Hotel with Dan, Jon and Myself. They look good..Ben too thin....walked to Circle in Square where we met Robert and all saw Shaw's Arms and The Man, Manhattan Ocean Club for fancy seafood dinner..." 13th,"Took Ben and Carol to

airport. Too short a visit. At least Rob looks peppier by afternoon. He missed the bombing by MOVE in Philly by being home..thank God."

May 29th,"Senior Awards Nite..Jon given plaque for Theatre Recognition..his Merit Finalist and graduate with distinction awards. Made him big chocolate cake in his honor. Dan and I thrilled again by our son..a sweet person as well as bright and generous." 31st,"Evening of Comedy a wonderful show! Beautiful introduction written by Jon. Big hit..everyone loved it..very professional".

June 1st," large happy audience both nites. He drove car to cast party...home at 2 a.m. (This is it!)". 13th,"Ben's 28th birthday. Bless him. All called him to sing Happy Birthday". 25th," Great to not have to arise at 6 am anymore for school bus...ever! We all plan a couple of days in NYC for shows and museums and a drive to Lakewood for visit with grandparents.

Dec. 19 to 22nd," Happy days, Jonathan home, feels normal and real. Made Hanukah meal, gave Jon new bongo drum set. House is lively and Jon getting lot of sleep, piano playing of his Godspell songs, seeing his old school friends, on Fri. and Sat. no vertigo. Ordered tkts. for Edwin Drood, Alvin Ailey Dancers, and Jerry's Girls for the week..Had wonderful day in city..went to Met Museum ..saw St. Gaudens and Kensett exhibits . Had vertigo at night and next day again, possibly due to overtired, crowds, driving at night, low barometer?".

13th,"Dr. Haynes visit, took me off Diazide, to continue for 1 month on Cyclospasm"

The other entries in this particular MOMA diary booklet went on as usual, and was glad to finish after a while, once we had the 'empty nest'. Not to worry, as there are a couple more books around 1992 to 1996 with descriptions of some of our trips camping adventures once we got our adorable puppy basset-hound called Tippy, or to make a very short and quite long story, actually named Tipette Fromage. (She loved to eat cheese....fast forward...she died at 12 years old....few years later we adopted a shelter dog, border collie mix called Princess at her age 2 ½ years and she has Tippy's spirit within her always and she loves cheese!)

Two other very pretty books held assorted diaries, sketchy notes as well as very long descriptions of several trips, one little book has Victoriana Diary 1994 on cover and all the pages have pretty little Victorian drawings and pictures with old-fashioned dress and images throughout. Used for brief notes now and then, and left many blank pages...of importance noted for Dec. 1993 "Family Hanukkah at JCC in NJ at Carol and Ben's, all came, young Sonia and Josh and Sasha and Jon and Joan whose wedding was end of November1993" and 31st,"Carol visits with Sonia and Joshua..Sonia stays over for a few days..Robert, Melanie and Sasha visit..we toast New Year's Eve..Sonia bakes a big NY Eve cake for us" and 1st "play chess, games, pancke breakfast" and 2nd,"we take Sonia home to NJ'. And skipping to Jan 31st "awful cold and ice storms and heavy snows this winter...18 storms...worse in years" February 9,"Daisy dies am in Paul Kimble Hospital, Lakewood NJ, heart failure, esophageal cncer spread to abdomen" 10th "Storm" 11th,"Dr appt. NYC...horrible snow storm...LIRR stops..stayed over at Ben's..called Jonathan for his birthday". Feb 21st-22nd "Carol brings Sonia and Joshua to stay few days while she flies to Boston meeting..lots of snow, lots of fun with kids". March 8th,"leave for trip to North Carolina, stay over at Gettysburg, snow covered battlefield". Mar. 9th"visit Eisenhower home and farm, very worthwhile..no tourists " March 10th to 16th," vacation South (by car with Tippy) see Gen Marshall Museum..Wilson's birthplace Staunton..Carl Sandburg's farm..Biltmore Estate...Blue Ridge Mtns had green grass..below Roanoke..driving with Tippy worked out fine..home by 2 pm on LI 16th". More details about this trip in severe winter of 1994 were written on other sheets, March 8, "stayed in Gettysburg, PA our first day out of LI, we drove about 7 hours with an obliging Tippy to our 1st stop, en route to Asheville. Much thick white fog along Penn Tpke near Lancaster, about 6 pm we had a beautiful drive through the Gettysburg Battlefield, covered with white snow, which etched the rocks, hills, monuments clearly and was a good way to gain another quiet impression after our first visit when it was crowded and hot last July. We had a restful evening in Quality Inn and made breakfast in our room. Mar. 9 Stayed in Lexington, VA, woke to snowing weather and are worried that we can't take the tour of the Eisenhower Farm and House. We were in great luck as we could see the electric map, a worthwhile description of the 3 days of battle, in the Visitor Center and then tour the Eisenhower house with guide. This was very interesting and with only 3 tourists, we had a very personalized chance to ask questions and see the rooms with the Ranger having time to do anecdotes. Then we drove to Lexington VA along past beautiful Harpers Ferry area and then down (rather boring in the rain and sleet) I-81. Had a restorative evening rest and now...(Mar. 10 Stayed over in Abingdon, VA) are off to see Geo. Marshall Museum,(of Marshall Plan) WW 2 museum and all about him and that era in history. Also Stonewall Jackson's house in Lexington. Our goal is to get to Asheville tomorrow to see Biltmore Estate, Thos. Wolfe home (did not see this) and Sandburg's farm in that area, for a few days. Then we will return hopeful (I must be getting tired and scared of the weather and all the driving) via West VA to see the glass works there(we couldn't get to that). Tippy had her dog license and rabies tag lost yesterday...very aggravating. We finally found all 3 from her collar out in snow. The Marshall Museum on ground of beautiful old (before Civil War) Virginia Military Institute, VMI, was very worthwhile and impressive to see with a WW1 and WW2 re-education. Mar. 13, Enjoyed visit to Sandburg house, I toured indoors and up to attic study while Tippy and Dan strolled the farm to see hills and the goats that Mrs. Sandburg kept. Then we drove to Abingdon, VA, at last seeing GREEN GRASS and signs of spring, especially past Roanoke. Mar. 11 heading to Asheville, stayed over in Gaitlenberg, too touristy, pretty locale. mar. 12 We had leisurely visit to the breathtaking forest and gardens of Biltmore and saw the castle there, had lunch in the converted old stable. Big place. Big fee. (usual garden plantings not done yet due to too cold weather)Mar. 15 had a good rest overnite in Hendersonville, took rt. 40 drive for view of Smokies. After yesterday driving to mtns. on 221 to see real foothill country style, we stayed over in Marion. Today, up 40 and now on pretty 16 in sunshine, fields plowed, forsythia in bloom, lots of open farms and clear outlines of repeating blue ridge mtns. straight ahead. Never have to walk far in these highlands to find a Baptist church. Went up onto Blue Ridge Pkwy. Beautiful drive, some scenic stops, some stretches were pretty scary turns around ice-clad cliffs with sheer drops. stone mtn. area. then off it to rt. 21 and up north on VA side, to Wytheville, very hilly drive, farms, small and poor villages, lots of cows. now to I-81 north to Staunton to visit Woodrow Wilson birthplace and museum tomorrow. Went through Mt. Rogers Natl. Forest, almost had a downing tree fall on our car as the men at work told us to pass under the tree being sawed down. Missed us by a few yards. Mar. 15 Had nice rest last night in cozy place in Salem VA, few thousand more calories at Shoneys, then beautiful driv e through foothills to Shenandoah Valley area.....Staunton...Tippy doing real fine on all of trip, so far. Saw snow again when north of Roanoke, but not too much of it... mar 16 long drive directly home to LI, worked out well and glad to see our house still standing. Next couple of days catching u on chores, 2 more snowfalls, but light ones. The echoing mtn. silhouettes of Blue Ridge are a great memory, as are several of the historic spots we learned more about.

To return from this diversion from Victoriana, there are a few more entries in this pretty book which might be mentioned, as in May 2nd to May 11th," Went on trip to Vermont, Brattleboro, Rutland, Proctor Marble Museum, overnite near Middlebury, Saw Morgan Horse Farm, crossed Lake Champlain to Keene, Lake Placid, Beautiful bridge and mtn. scenery around lake, stayed in North Adirondacks few days, Paul Smiths Nature center toured, drove to Newcomb Nature Ctr. near Long Lake, Glen Falls, enjoyed all this a lot, to Bennington, Manchester, Vermont, Berkshire home on ferry, refreshing trip for Dan, Tippy, Mitzi, home, fix up jobs around house and garden in Stony Brook." June 8 to 15,"went to Ben and Carol's house to child sit while they go to Sweden, lots of fun with Sonia and Joshua for the week there, they had a good trip to the medical meeting in Stockholm, all safe and well". July11 for 3 weeks, went on our camping trip to Nova Scotia and Newfoundland, did 3,000 miles," had wonderful time, Tippy came along too". Then Aug 19th "Jonathan completed his law clerk job, 2 years, today." Aug. 20th,"Dan flew to Dallas on business trip". No more entries in pretty Victoriana book, with the pictures of Circus toys ,baby bonnets, Santa Claus shops with old-fashioned items, and so forth. Very, very RETRO. Even moreso, now that it is saved since THEN in 1994, up to NOW at least, in 2008.

Another little book with scene of Venice gondolas on cover, has some notes from 1992 to 1996. The entries were brief and few and far between, so these highlights will not tax one's finger joints to type or one's eyeballs to scan. Sadly Jan. 4, 1992 was our last visit to be with my old friend Gloria Friedman Franklin, before she succumbed to cancer. She and Gerry and children lived always in NYC, and we shared many events and beach days and so forth with them. I was their note passing friend back in graduate school Psychology class, as I sat between them and enabled their early courtship. Gerry always had his beloved German Shepard dog with him, sitting in class. Various med appts. scattered over the months. Jan 23 we went to museum at 12 and had dinner at 5:30 with Jonathan in 57th st. Spanish restaurant, Jonathan
was by then at Columbia Law School. Feb. 18 we took Tippy to the Hauppauge Vet and she weighed 10 lbs. Noted that Joshua at 3 mos. weighed 15 lbs. and was 26 ¾ in. tall, as Carol reported. Noted visits with Dr. Nastasi, Dr. Dowd, piano tuner Klepack, bot Explorer on April 20, shortly after the Moot Court at Columbia Law School where Jonathan won best written brief, to our great pride. That
week he was also in the Show at the Law School, and Apr. 26 we attended Lenny and Sylvia's 50th anniv. party in NJ and saw many of my other Germansky relatives many now passed away. May 13 Jon graduated from Law School, went to Sonia's school at 2 pm in NJ, and on June 10, Robert and Melanie were married in the Temple, with their

celebration in Conn. a few days later., and Jon was best man, Ben had birthday the 13th and Sonia was a cute little girl and Josh attended in his stroller.. July 28 Jon had his NY State bar exams and Aug. 1 moved to Baltimore for his clerkship.By Sept,.I was seeing orthoped. Dr. Kurtz for my bad back, and a check up with gyn. Dr. Lapid, who I knew for ever it seems. Nov. and Dec. were med, chimney cleaning, museum exhibits, minor surgeries, and most important of all, Nov. 6 at 9 a.m. Tippy had her nails clipped! So there you go. I am saving the artistic book of Hiroshige but am happy to now tear up the pages of appointments and events.

Not all of this could be so simple I see. My book with the Venetian front cover holds loads of words from some of our travels, 1992, 1995, 1996, and a few souvenirs, as the Passamaquoddy Park in St. Andrews, New Brunswick, Canada camping pass, the Sherwoo Forest in New Harbor, Maine camping pass, Ford Explorer license #K9J282,(I think the K9..was precient for Tippy's presence in the trailer) the Shady Oaks Campground in Bucksport, Maine pass, date in 8-21-92 and date out 8-22-92 for $12.84 These receipts help prove that all the writing is not based only on fantasy. l f not adequate proof, please note that in Passamaquoddy Park we were on Site No. 84 and the Park Attendant signed name as Amy.

August 20, 1992, approximately 2 weeks, trip written about in ink, as....Wed day out of Stony Brook we are camping at Pemaquid Beach near Damariscotta Maine. Tippy is adored by many folks on trip up, and she is a good camper-doggie. Dan is busy setting up our Coleman trailer under the pine trees. Air is crisp and cool...the water look great along the coast. I get provisions ready for our cook-out tonight. lst night we styed at Port Motel in Portsmouth, NH. Fine place. Sherwood Forest camp...good location for gorgeous view of Pemaquid Lighthouse and Henry Fort. Tippy a hit with lots of people.(they didn't have to take care of her...just look and giggle) Enjoyed our cold night in camper. Friday set out north after breaking camp. Passed beautiful Camden area, had picnic lunch, crossed steep Penobscot River at the old iron bridge, decided to stay at campground under Shady Oaks, nice pool. Had great pancakes and coffee for breakfast in the camper. Took off to NE. Scenic and lovely, especially our Schoodic Point drive in Acadia Natl. Park, a gorgeous coastline overlooking Frenchman's Bay, past Bar Harbor. Town of Winter Harbor, just before the one-way loop drive. Tippy loved climbing on the rocks at coastline and drinking from the pools of water left by rain near the beach. Sunday, drove along Passamaquoddy Bay to Machias and Calais..after one night's rest and shower in a motel near Campobello. Entered Canada at New Brunswick after food shopping and breakfast in Calais, to insulate ourselves for the camping in Canada Behold! We had pleasant time in NB and found beautiful spot at St. Andrews overlooking a Fundy arm. Quoddy Loop. Decided to camp and stay 2 nights to relax. Sea breezes waft over camper. Had long walk at low tide along beach. Tippy loves it, found lobsters (red ones) to play with.

Monday,"took our morning walk from the camp ground, into St. Andrews and back. up and down their main street which has many tourist shops, food shops. The town is very clean, pleasant and quiet with little houses that date back to 1780when British loyalists left Maine and moved to this area. The local folk seem to be people of few

words. But they often are attracted to Tippy and ask if they can pet her. They are very impressed by her beauty and friendliness. (These are Dan's words). after we went to Katy's Cove where we swam in Bay of Fundy at low, low tide. The water was warm..Tippy ..lot of attention and petting…a real compliment to Mitzi's care of Tippy. (Hey, these are Dan's written words, so this whole long excrutiating process of printing
the old diaries has finally paid off for me, as I did get a compliment for my care…what about the other caring…kids, hubby, in-laws, etc.) Today has been a langorous, lazy day, wonderful after a few days of road work."(well when he said road work, it wasn't digging ditches and putting up red flags, but driving a lot which is a wonderful accomplishment of Dan, always) Back to my writing for Tues. "Lovely drive in marvelous vast hilly coastline from St. Andrews all the way to Fundy Natl. Park. . . Stopped at St. Johns, oldest Incorporated town in Canada, to see the Martello Stone Tower overlooking city, built 1812. Had good tail-gate picnic high on blueberry hill, rt. 411? off of #2..going to Fundy. Great fun. Dan is great driver. First night in uncrowded Park, we sty at a motor inn at edge of sea…now at low tide we could walk out forever…..but.not for long, when tide rushes in soon. Wed. drive in the Park to see the covered bridge and scenery at Wolfe's Point, then lunched on chowders and sandwiches in the Chalet Restaurant, and drove on to "the rocks."..Thurs. Lone Pine Camp proved a great solution after a long day's drive up to see the stupendous Rocks and then past Moncton, rt. 114 and rt 2 again. We had a refreshing quiet sleep in the little camper, with dinner and pancake breakfast cooked there. The gravel covered site was neat too. At the "rocks" we took a long walk with Tippy scampering all along the shores at low tide. The stupendous formations, with tree lines high above, were worth the trip to NB. Reminds us of Monument Valley in Arizona, seen previously with Jonathan years ago. All these caves and pinnacles get submerged twice a day at high tide, only to pop up again. The river valley at low tide is all pinkish-red where banks are exposed. Lovely vast farms along the way too. That was Wednesday. Now we start towards Fredericton to follow St. John's River. May go to Hartland, boasting longest covered bridge, etc. Air cool and grey. Tippy had long run in the woods.

　　Approached Fredericton along the lovely river banks of St. Johns R. Stopped for berries, corn, apples at farm. Prosperous, vast dairy farms. Well kept fields. Road #2 curves beautifully close to the river banks, rows of trees, now deciduous, out of evergreen forests. Very esthetic drive. Fri. Crossed back to USA at Calais again. Bkfst. at very nice and busy alais Motor Inn again. Then ride along Maine inland forest Rt. 9, to Bangor and Skowhegan, looking to camp, as we prefer this to motels. Sat. Last night we recovered at the extremely comfortable Best Western in Augusta, Maine, after driving from Calais, across lovely, isolated mountainside country in Maine, down to Belgrade Lakes, then Augusta. Today, after Rt. 1 along Maine seacoast, which is too jammed up and crowded to stay at, we go inland again on rt. 101, in NH, towards Manchester. Almost stopped at 3 Ponds Campsite, which was l mile in, according to sign. But, lo and behold, a huge correctional institution then loomed on the dirt road,(used to call a prison or jailhouse), after a few charming farms. Decided not to stay overnite. NH should have marked this on the road sign, why the mystery? Settled in at Ramada Inn in Keene, after gorgeous scenery, drive past Monadnock State Park. Hope to camp tomorrow in Green Mtns of Vermont?"

"Drive across Connecticut R. to Brattleboro and Green Mtns. Found a great campsite called Country Aire on Rt. #2, the Mohawk Trail. Wide grassy site,surrounded by mountains, a pool and loads of relaxing fresh air. Dan got his red hatchet at a flea market en route and built an evening fire. We did turkey and marshmallows. Relaxing couple of days for us here, before returning home. Mon. We relaxed at campsite, cooked pancakes, veggies, noodles. Went to Bridge of Flowers at Shelburne Falls for diversion. Would not allow Tippy to walk on path there however. Swam. Had fun outdoor fire in evening, cold night, made midnight snack of pea-soup and campfire toast. Tippy snuggled under blankets for warmth. Clear starry night. Tues. Woke to go back to sleep until 8:30. Made coffee and campfire toast. Tippy had her white meat chicken breakfast from can. Took another swim before breaking camp. Head to Ferry and home. Gorgeous open sunny field in mountains. Goodbye—till again. (Note that years later the Country Aire Campsite could not be found, went out of business.)We left at 11:30 a.m. Tuesday. Drove through beauties of Mohawk Valley, all tall green mtns, lovely road, quiet, views of Berkshires all about. then Rt. 37 at North Adams, down towards Lenox. Had a good civilized luncheon in Lenox, browsed some stores, got Dan his sweat pants and turtleneck, for next camping trip.   We had a 7:30 Ferry reservation in Bridgeport. But, in spite of many pit stops along the way, we pulled in
to ferry road at 5:59, just as the 6:00 pm ferry was loosening ties. They waved us to drive on, so we made it, with just one-inch to spare, trailer and car! Had, therefore, an earlier crossing in nice weather. Tippy was so excited. We stayed below, and Dan brought her a hamburger, which she devoured happily. So---it's been a lucky trip, fun, an adventure camping and traveling with our Basset-Hound, who made it happily and in good health to Bay of Fundy Park---and home. Just two weeks exactly, and 1,670 miles! It has been refreshing!   "

As a NOW remark, July 2008, let us calculate the cost of gas for this trip at current much higher rates, forbidding rates actually.At roughly 15mpg, and NOW cost of about $4.50 per gallon,would be much more expensive to drive, and this
does not include the tolls and wear and tear on auto and trailer, so it would cost much more for the traveling. The campsite and motel fees not included in this, nor the food, incidentals, but now the food enroute is much more expensive, because no "box stores" en route.Then there was, a much stronger dollar and much better exchange rate to Canadian dollar. Their fuel
however was always more than here, at that time.   Oh well, glad we did do it when we did do it……..ain't you?

As necessary when traveling, occasional restorative intervals were necessary, and now, as traveling along memory lane in this book with Venetian gondolas on cover, it is advisable to take a much needed rest. About 6 or 7 handwritten pages follow and will go to 1994, 1993, 1996, and grow more and more staccato in beat with long pauses between and lots of repeat lines, as in Franz Schubert's music. so take a break.

Early September-Spent few days getting things in order at home…mail, laundry, banking, etcetera. Vow to take off on another great camping trip very soon.

1993- Summer- Spent several short stays at LI Eastern Campgrounds near Orient Point. Easy drive out. relaxing getaway. ..walks at beach, fish dinners, pool swims…biggest trip of this summer was on July 4 weekend –to Maryland and Pennsylvania…to see Jonathan and Joan, who became engaged. We explored civil war sites…Antietam, Gettysburg, Harper's Ferry…very, very hot spell but interesting

We are planning for a long time to drive across country and see Inside Passage of Alaska and then drive back east through Canada. As of January, 1994, we have reserved space on the Ferry from Bellingham Washington to Juneau, Alaska—leaving May 13. We must start our auto trip west around April 13.to see some sights and cover the miles. Elsewhere this fantastic trip can be described. The Inner Passage of Alaska was great to see with the ferry enabling us to stop over at will in different ports for as long as we desired and then continue on with another ferry. Tippy traveled well. We got home by mid June from this long trip back and forth from East to West to East.

June 25-27 - Took Sonia camping at East End LI, fun for all. She learned a lot, enjoyed other kids, collected sea-shells, nice break for her after her lst grade school class ended. July 4 weekend-Just Dan and I and dog will again camp at LI Kampgrounds in Greenport, before our big summer trip, later in July, to Nova Scotia.

July 11 to July 31, 1994, 20 day trip…Had great travels to Nova Scotia and Newfoundland with Dan and Tippy, with our camper. Saw highland games at Antigonish and Western Brook Pond Fjord Boat at Gros Morne Natl. Park in NF

Spring 1995..Drove across to Bellingham, inside passage, Alaska, drove back East.

Summer 1995 July camped at NH and VT after trip to Alaska. Camped in Quechee Gorge, VT and Brattleboro, VT

On August 6 we took a 2 week trip, 1996. Our 44th anniversary trip. lv. on Ferry from Orient point to New London (not the Port Jeff ferry for a change) drive to Portsmouth NH, nice trip across, very hot weather. Aug 7 and 8 Drive north to Maine. stop at Rachel Carson Wildlife refuge to take the l mile walk through pretty woods near salt marsh. Tippy loved the exercise along the wooden walkways. Area very sparse in birds however. . another tourist wrote in the book at end of walk 'saw a chipmunk and a dachsund'. Likewise, and also, a Bassett ….scenic cool drive, picnic at rest stop, camp at #15 in Sherwood Forest. Good ice-cream in New Harbor. Beautiful fig in a.m., drove to the lighthouse. stayed at Pemaquid Point all morning. picnic. lucky us…the Morris Dancer performed there overlooking the sea. very lovely and much appreciated by the folks there. later we stopped at the Shaw's wharf to see scene. after a rest, we enjoyed being at historic Pemaquid Park where old fort and houses were, pretty view of whole bay…dinner outdoors at the restaurant overlooking waters, boats, islands. ..leave early Aug. 9 for Bucksport area. ..next time will try a different campground near Damariscotta.. past Rockland, bigger town, Camden, stopped to see Ferry to island in Penobscot bay, lunch near high bridge before Bucksport overlooking a river, which goes up from Bangor, like our Whispering Pines Campsite . in tall pines, on Toddy Pond, clean place and quiet, would recommend it. We drove next day to Blue Hill, bridge to Deer Island, bkfst at Bridge Inn spent restful time along sandy salt water beach there. (birds sighted by Dan, as Great Cormorant at Blue Hill, Black Ring Beak Seagull at Deer Isle, American Red Start at Nature Center in Acadia Park) Back at campsite..Dan made big fire in ring, we cooked: 3 corn, 3 carrots, 4 pieces chickent, beef liver for Tippy and a wonderful fresh fish called Cusp something like haddock, firm, tasty, in evening. will drive tomorrow to Ellsworth and then be at Acadia for 3 days, at Smuggler's Den Camp in Southwest Harbor. Very good weather today, although last night had a rainstorm, but no problem from it at all…except too many mosquitoes. p. s. Glad to hear that Dole chose Kemp as his running mate today."

"unday..settled in camp, took swim in pool, lunched outdoors, rested up..drove to see Bass Harbor Headlight, past beautiful seal wall beach, bass harbor…long vistas of ocean and rocky island..had soft'shell lobster dinner in town…cold at night, used heater plus sleeping bags in camper. Note that Rockland, ME is birthplace of Edna St. Vincent Millay, poet and of Walter Piston, composer.. Monday..made pancakes with blueberry syrup..drove to visitor center of Acadia Park to get tape, ranger orientation talk, etc. ..crowded there (happened to meet Sasha's little friend Bobby Ulman and family there and talked a while together.) Started tour. Vista of Porcupine Islands. Took turn towards Bubble Pond..beautiful walk in woods there near lake..drove to Bubble Rock area, walked part way up, steep, rocky path. …went for lunch at Northeast Harbor,(where the home of Morison, historian and sailor is), ~~in old, elegant~~ Strolled at pretty harbor, drove to Bar Harbor, stopping at Soeur de Mont Nature Center, walked in 'wildflower garden' of ferns, mosses, heaths…passed Jackson Laboratory but missed lecture there, picking up some folders..drive across center, Rt. 233, good views, to return to campsite. nice quiet camp…made dinner inside camper, and relaxed…cold night. The elegant Inn in Northeast Harbor was called the Asticou Inn…one of the last two inns from the late 1800s..we had our lunch on an outdoor terrace overlooking the harbor and the garden which had arbor vitae shaped like candelabrs and an oriental thich big carpet in the ladies' restroom, as appreciated by Mitzi…..Aug. 13. decided to relax and see harborsides instead of another crowded 'loop tour' as we have seen all of that plus criss-crossed Mt. Desert Island, both sides, a few times already. after pancakes, we set out for Southwest Harbor and Bass Harbor again, strolled around slowly, had picnic on rocks of the seawall…afternoon did laundry, had beef-stew made in camper and tidied up for tomorrow's trip to Oceanwood at Schoodic Point…other part of Acadia Pk. near Winter Harbor..did not stay there as we did not like the looks of that Oceanwood Camp. Returned home via Bangor, Augusta, where we did overnite at Augusta motel, then crossed by ferry to Orient Point late at night, dark and starry , and drove home listening to Dole's

acceptance speech in California at the Republican Natl. Convention, Aug. 14.   (p. s.
Dole lost that election).

Sorry that Dole lost, but glad that all the pages leading to this printing job can
now be tossed out to clear the shelves, while their content is not lost. The Venetian
Gondola book can still hang around for a while, if needed for future entries.
Well, it is not the ultimate WAY BACK THEN which will go to the late 19th and very
early 20[tth] century background of memories, a la geneology records and stories, but
actually it is sort of half of WAY BACK THEN by now to dig up stuff from near 1945,
when I graduated from Weequahic High School, and some college years and some years
of early motherhood with children growing from little to big, so with the year book
called Legend, 1945 Class open to the story called '...In Our Time' the dramatic era of
WW2 which was our adolescence. a classmate wrote. 'December 7, 1941, with its
undying echoes and reverberations of exploding bombs, zooming planes, moaning of
wounded, and the other audible heralds of war, found us, the June 1945 class of
Weequahic High, just embarking on our high school careers. Three months previous we
had entered the Annex as a group of literal freshmen with brave hearts, high hopes, and
hidden fears. Now after our period of indoctrination, we were all at home at the
Annex.....etc. but many changes were effected in our daily lives at school. Preparations
for efficient air raid drills were begun at the time that the Philippines, Wake, and other
Pacific islands were being bombed unrelentlessly. Wake Island fell to the Japs, on
December 23, as we began our first war time Christmas vacation. Upon return to school,
we faced our first H.S. exams... they fell this time in revenge on Tokyo iself...General
Doolittle's flyers from the carrier Hornet...the announcement of the fall of Singapore,
Bataan, Corregidor...the great naval victories of the Coral Sea and Midway...there is no
doubt that Weequahic was a H.S. at war...courses in aeronautics, radio
communications..first aid..Victory Corps, collection of newspapers, tin foil and tooth
paste tubes..90% participation in purchase of War Bonds and Stamps earning the
Minutenman Flag for school...glee club and school band Stamp Parades....on October
17, 1942 the House of Representatives passed a bill lowering the draft age to
eighteen.....called some of the boys in their senior year at that time...(I took Military
German Class) landings in North Africa on Nov. 7...Casablanca conference demanded
for unconditional surrender...when we entered 1A..the Russians turned the course of the
war on their front by turning back the Nazis at Stalingrad..when the annual Music Review
came to Weequahic, Churchill also came to Washington..there was 10 o'clock curfew
requiring age 16 or younger be off the streets ...Dr. Melnik and Weequahic Band got
music award presented by the leader of the West Point Band......the Honor Society held
event in NY where Paul Robeson portrayed Othello..on June 7 every radio utilized in
school to bring the news of the Allied invasion of France..difficult it was to concentrate
upon past history when it was in the making at that very moment...Mr. Roosevelt's re-
election was anticipated by many of us...what was not anticipated was the President's
sudden death on April 12, 1945..mourning throughout....our generation had lost its
greatest leader...long after Berlin occupied by the Allies..May 7 students of Weequahic
High, ears glued to the radio, heard President Truman officially proclaim V-E Day...our
Class of 1945..lived through four years of war and high school simultaneously.'
Reading this today, I am again impressed with how mature we had to become while in

High School, and how wonderful the writing was, to preserve the events up to NOW. Preserved in this yearbook, are the tassel from my graduation cap,
photo from Bragaw Ave. School elem. class,, most of those went on
to Weequahic High School, letters from Dave Horwitz who to this day in 2008 still keeps the class members up to date with what happened to each over the years, their grandchildren, their careers, the obituaries, etc..And some of my later events, in college at Cornell U. and Grad. School at NYU, and School Psychologist Certificate, and copy of my paper on Rorschach Ph. D. thesis in Perceptual and Motor Skills, 1959 which was published before birth of my first son, Benjamin Tycko, now Pathology Prof. at Columbia U.. Many of these souvenirs are saved in the mail folder. The Legend 60 Years Later, re. 60th Reunion, is saved with the class of 1945 Yearbook.

In the stash of papers still saved, are also Meeting of.. Physical Society 2005 prize and award
booklet with son Robert getting Plyer prize, also a copy of son Jonathan's appearance to Supreme Court of the United States as Counsel of Record #00-1168,Class of 1992 Grad. Ceremonies School of Law, Columbia U. for Jonathan's degree ,many scientific articles published or spoken at meetings by both sons, Benjamin and Robert, play copyright 1994 called The Inside by Jonathan,, and of course copies of my husband Daniel's many science papers, theses of Rob, Ben, Dan and Myself…and the list goes on in case anyone want to know. What remains NOW are myriad images and memories of all these events and family people surrounding them, as grandparents, uncle Arnold, friends of yore, many deceased and many still breathing, if not in places easily identified.

So, other than having to finally cope with the real WAY BACK THEN papers and stories, which seems to be definitely a forbidding task, these pages above will have to suffice as a summary of THEN, half of WAY BACK THEN, some of NOW.
A bunch of poems, stories, impressions from over the decades are probably much more interesting for deeper content, and are not included in this WORD Document.but rather in a booklet called The Old Lacquered Box..

P. S. perhaps a large monetary award will have to be promised to anyone who dares to start and finish successfully the reading of the above.

WAY BACK THEN

I took a short course in our local Emma Clark Library a few years ago
One of the nice librarians guided us through many of the references
that could be used to create our own Genealogy booklet. luckily we
took these several sessions, because by now this is no longer offered
at the library. I looked up so many interesting things, from the passenger
lists of my grandparents coming to Ellis Island, to whereabouts of other
relatives who came then, to what happened to the various ships later on,
and this had inspired me to get many of the old black and white photos of
my 'ancestors' and try to identify their siblings and cousins, and to
interview some of my own cousins who had their memories to supplement
mine. This ended up forming a very large loose-leaf notebook full of stuff.
Also this ended up on some floppy discs
    Already a few of the younger relatives have passed away, but I did
locate their own grandchildren. A brief summary of the Leichtling and
the Germansky backgrounds is here, but the actual
pages from the huge notebook will have to be scanned and copied at
a later date....perhaps in the local Staples store which handled some
other writings for me recently.. Boy oh boy.....I have given myself another
grueling job, but in the long run it may serve to make it useful for
our own grandchildren and theirs way down the road. Not sure if this
will be a paved road or a rutted dirt road in future, because NOW the
world situation is filled with dangers from terrorists. Not really analogous,
but looking back on my grandparents' emigration from countries
becoming dangerous in world wars, history repeatedly occurs and dangerous history
occurs, although wonderful, happy history occurs also....though not repeating in all
the details. Enough said.
    Since one of my aunts, Serena Leichtling ,daughter of Adolf and Minnie Leichtling,
my grandparents who came to Ellis Island from Austro-Hungarian empire in 1900, ended
up living in Greece during most of her adult life, it shows that to adequately understand
the history of WAY BACK THEN we have to study ancient Greece and read in
Greek those famous writers. And we will be ignorant of what happened in 19th
century Austria, whatever the changing boundaries were, unless we go further
back in European history. Of course, the area around Odessa in the Ukraine, which
housed my grandparents, Germanskys, in the Jewish communities there can
be traced back thousands of years at least to all the wanderings of Jews from Palestine,
the limited part of their journeys that surround the Black Sea, let alone to
China and even Australia (See Patrick White's novels.)
    Limit we must, for sanities sake, in
referencing some of the WAY BACK THEN. Actually I did read several novelists
and historians to help form the genealogy notebook. These will be described moreso
when the genealogy notebook is copied.
    It was i a very challenging moment to dig up material, because photographs
and other records were so limited, , sparse Internet access and if any.family photos
could be found,it was a boon. If the photographer's name and place were scripted on

the back of the old black and white photos, that was a boon too

For the coming generations there is an overwhelming mass of images and historical records available on the Internet, so it is probably misguided of me to think that my descendants could be as delighted as I was to find any grains of old history. Lucky we were, in taking the brief library course, to come across some new ways of finding things, and everyone in the sessions was excited that they could trace some previously unknown family mysteries.

With some help from my husband's cousin, I also could trace back some of the history of the Sadicoff and Tyckochinski background. from Russia and Poland respectfully.

The ships carrying my ancestors , whose names are on Passenger Lists, with dates and what happened to the ships later on, will follow:

Adolf Leichtling came on The Spaarndam from Rotterdam (he had lived in Rohatyn, Austria) at age of 32 years, arriving at Ellis Island August 21, 1900.This ship built 1881 in Ireland,various other owners, was scrapped in England in 1901. Adolf just made it in 1900. Minni, his wife, followed later.

Dwoire Germanski, age 40 years, and her children (my father Yossel, Joseph) arrived in Ellis Island on August 06, 1912 on ship called The Campanello, built in Newcastle, England in 1902, various owners, torpedoed and sunk by a German sub in 1918. They had lived in St. Constantinou near to Odessa, Russia. My Zayde, Ausher Germanski died previously in Russia of pneumonia. Fortunate, to put it mildly, to escape Europe on The Campanello well before the German sub bombing and the German Nazi onslaught. As I note for the first time NOW that The Spaarndam was scrapped in England in 1901, while The Campanello was built England in 1902, this sequence seems more than coincidental and may tell about the business of shipbuilding in that country. Good topic for naval historians. First my maternal grandfather and then 12 years later my paternal grandmother and children were carried on British ships to Ellis Island.

The white notebook with loads of records, photos, interesting stories,which was my project in 2002 – 2003, has pages measuring over one and a half inches when stacked.

Not to elaborate further in this short introduction to WAY BACK THEN, and only to say in NOW that I was just very moved to glance again at all the photos and stories about my relatives, more since passed away, and I feel it will be a very time-consuming, difficult, almost onerous job to stick with my commitment to have the pages scanned and put into a few copied genealog y booklets….however there are worse commitments people have. I am graced by having my husband Daniel nearby, who will no doubt be glad to help with the sorting out and driving to Staples that will be involved.

This is dependent on weather also because our adorable adopted border come mix called Princess will cooperate only when the day is not overly hot and muggy. She has proven hat she, at least, is very interested in these pages, because she enjoys mouthing the notebook and sniffing it and lying quietly nearby while I work my way along with the computer. This is vitally encouraging….to know that at least someone does care about the hassle involved. Maybe it will be done before her third birthday on August 14, 2008.. That would be a nice birthday present for all of us. I will buy her a vanilla ice-cream cone.

and we certainly did buy Princess vanilla ice-cream cones, in fact several, which were also enjoyed a week or so later when grandchildren Arielle and Serena (ages 7 and 9) visited to play with her... and their parents Jonathan and Joan helped us celebrate our 56th anniversary .... a delicious box of Godiva chocolates .... all of us enjoyed .... not the doggie because chocolate is poison to dogs .... extra petting for Princess baby

M Y

P.S. The Genealogy books were given to Jonathan and also to granddaughter Sonia when she visited on returning from her summer doing research in London, UK.

(-16-)

NOW

or… Genealogy……..oi.. gevalt

This morning, feeling a slight sense of accomplishment, because yesterday
I did manage to sort out many pages and photos of my 2003 Genealogy report,
I walked over boldly to my desk. It had remnants of yesterday's work
strewn aabout, just begging to continue being sorted out intelligently. But
I could only feel……oi..gevalt!   Yesterday'.s pages were neatly numbered
up to 40.. Looked fairly simple to continue on, however the rest of the pages
scattered helter-skelter on my desk belied any naïve idea that the process would
go on easily. As a brief example of the papers scattered about, were:
A small note of "to-do" chores: Cyndi's List-1910 and 1920 census for
naturalization status; 1930 census in Ancestry.com; need DISPLAY to work; NY State
Census for 1925, 1915; FEEFHS map room; all research tools but on such a tiny
slip of paper that it would necessitate scanning and printing on to a notebook size
sheet to use…so instead I just mention this now and let myself skip doing the
time consuming enlargement.
Next lay the Ellis Island Passenger Record for Leichtling, Adolf, Ethnicity Austria,
Place of Residence Rahatyn (their misspelling), Date of Arrival August 21, 1900,
age on Arrival 32y Gender M Marital status S,Ship Travel Spaardam Departure
Rotterdam, South Holland, The Netherlands.   Oh boy…..this is
indescribably important…Adolf was my maternal grandfather, young
man to be the earliest arriving of my ancestors from Europe to USA, my grandmother
Minnie arrived later with four of their children. My mother, Daisy Belle Leichtling was
born in New Jersey,as was her younger sister Sylvia..
So I am a second generation , and of course she graduated H.S., spoke English always,
and her parent s Leichtlings learned English and raised a family here successfully.
Adolf had served in the Austrian Cavalry as a "medical technician" accompanying
troops
on railway travels to Germany, etc. and wife Minnie accompanied. too. Although he
claimed to be Single on arrival here, he shortly after brought Minnie here also,
with their four children.. They eventually had
a total of six offspring, all to be noted further in the Genealogy notebook.
So there! The next piece of paper in the pile is actually rather important. Guess
what? It is the marriage license certificate of Joseph Germansky, age 29, birthplace
Russia, to Daisy B. Leichtling, age 24, birthplace United States, date January 30, 1928,
place of marriage Newark, N J, performed by Rabbi H. Brodsky, no. 4552.

Then another resources sheet for the genealogy search…Israellinks.asp on which are
many sites to help trace Jewish roots, such as the Galilee Genealogical Society, JFRA
Petah Tikva, Jewish Family Research Association and others, a sheet with small photo of
Jonathan's children. our grandbildren Serena and baby Arielle when very little. then
some E-mail messages saved from cousins who helped me put together the details,
mainly from Morkap@aol.com (he has since passed away) in 2003 and then a copy of a

-17-

newspaper article dated Oct. 6 Moscow, describing how Gorbachev Condemns An ti-Semitism, „ saying that "hatred of Jews still exists in everyday life, the Soviet leader acknowledges"Past and Present", at the Babi Yar memorial at edge of Kiev in the Ukraine. This was always an emotional review for me because my paternal grandparents left Ukraine (luckily) WAY BACK THEN in 1918;and Bubba Germanski and children went first to #42 at corner of Bellevue and Cortland St., in Belleville, NJ, to join Bubba's sister the Schreibers who came in 1912. Later, after doing this research, my husband Daniel and I,
joined by our pet dog Tippy, did go to visit that exact address. We found a large printing press factory now on that exact corner, and we strolled around Belleville and took photos. Still a very nice town, with nice library and small houses, and patriotic flags all around with a largely Phillipino population and others now. (See Danny Stiles raconteur about days there as he plays old music records on WNYC);the town is on what was called "second river", close to the Geo. Washington Bridge and closely tied to Manhattan. In the pile of papers,there is a copy of the Jewish Veteran, where an article called "Journey of a Belleville Lad" on p. 10 recounts much of the early Belleville background as written by this Belleville Lad who is Catholic and wrote this affectionate tribute in The Catholic Advocate, 2006, wherein he gives a rundown of early history in Spain when Jews and Muslims were expelled during the Inquisition, and recounts that the Vatican signed diplomatic agreement of recognition with Israel in December 1993., while the Moslems still publish defamatory stereotypes of the Jews..The Germanski family altered their name to be spelled Germansky, and all settled mostly in Newark and Elizabeth area.
How grateful we should be that these forefathers all left Europe before devastation.

It was very helpful when my cousin Alice (Leichtling-Eisenberg) Morley, close to me in age, looked up records of when her mother, Lillian, oldest of the Leichtling children, was born, in Zeitz, Germany. Alice also had many stories about some of the Texas cousins, children of Minnie's sister who settled in Galveston, TX. Some other cousins filled in a few items when I talked to them.

So this sample of papers in disorderly array has to now be arranged , along with the other plastic covered pages in the plump genealogy white notebook, to be numbered distinctly for printing up at Staples soon. I have promised myself to complete this task by August 14, Princess my doggie's third birthday, so we can celebrate by giving her a vanilla ice-cream cone.
In this booklet called THEN, WAY BACK THEN, and NOW I am including a few comments.....just to whet
your appetite. Do not forget that there may possibly be a large monetary reward for anyone who plows through all this verbiage in future.

As I copied over many of the old family photos, of course memories and emotions about the people were filling up my time. That is why such a detailed Genealogy report is more interesting than one of those software "family tree" graphics. Maybe the diagrams are appropriate for the Kings and Queens and offspring of royalty....but much too summarily a way to investigate one's own "roots". What is the point of doing all these studies, except to understand oneself moreso. I like to combine this Genealogy work up with more personal musings of my own, to be found in the poems and essays written over many years, as in" The Old Lacquered Box" "booklet I recently put together. and also the next booklet of writings which I should call "More Musings". . All this gathering up of verbal and visual "dust" is occupying my NOW.

Forge ahead!

(few days later)
I did forge ahead, and as of today, I have arranged and numbered 201 pages of records, text, and photos. No claim to total accuracy, and everyone else is invited to delve more deeply into the records and text I gathered back in 2002 to 2003. Passenger Lists have not been edited, so any other similar names or places could still serve as hints for the Genealogy of Germanski, Leichtling, Sadicoff, Tyckochinski (Tycko) History of areas and eras can always be amplified. So, be my guest!

We are off to Staples to have this all printed and bound into several booklets for next generations. Best of all, our adopted doggie "Princess" will have her third birthday soon, and since she lay patiently near the computer for days and days, I promised her a big VANILLA ICE CREAM CONE. if I finished by then.

     Bye now,
Mitzi

(Millicent Leichtling Germansky Tycko)

                              July 27, 2008